Strip Tubing

Fast and Fabulous Quilts using The Strip Tube Ruler™

DESIGNS BY:

Daniela Stout
Georgette Dell'Orco
and Susan Van Alyne from *The Quilt House, Inc.* of Gardnerville, Nevada

Table of Contents

Cozy Quilt Designs ™

Strip Tubing
Fast and Fabulous Quilts using ᵀʰᵉ Strip Tube Ruler™

Printed in the United States of America

Designs by :   Daniela Stout, Georgette Dell'Orco, Susan Van Alyne
Publisher: Daniela Stout

Strip Tubing
Item Number: CQD04006
ISBN: 978-0-9795316-5-1

ISBN: 978-0-9795316-5-1
51895

9 780979 531651

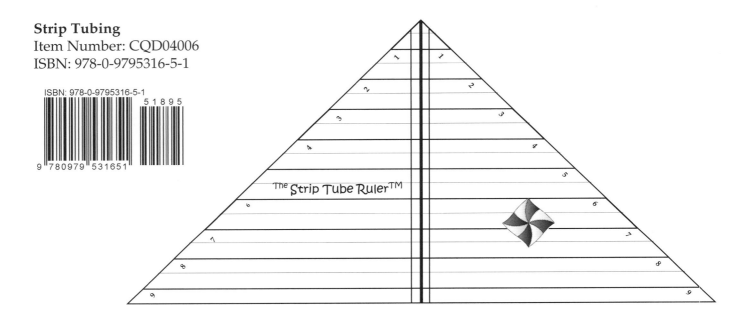

Welcome to the wonderful world of Strip Tubing! We've been using this technique for years, having great fun and making terrific quilts. Now it's your turn.

Before we begin, make your life easier by getting ᵀʰᵉ Strip Tube Ruler™ from your favorite quilt shop. This brilliantly designed ruler is a great addition to your quilting toolbox. You can use it over and over again.

Now that you have it… let's get to using it. If you don't have one, check out the next page for other directions.

The most difficult part is not that difficult! It's just a little different…. You have to make a tube. To do this you need two strips (or strip sets or combination of both). In our example below, we have a solid strip and a pieced strip of the same size. For more information on which size to use, see the patterns inside this book or the chart on the next page.

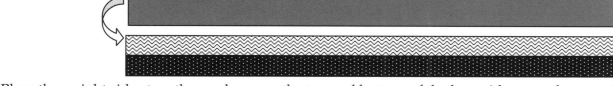

Place them right sides together and sew on the top and bottom of the long sides to make something that looks like a sleeve.. or a tube!

¼" seam on top and bottom

Then find the horizontal measurement of your unfinished block size on your ruler. Put that horizontal line on your bottom stitching line and cut up one diagonal side and down the other to get a triangle that opens to a square.

Trim off the dog ears, press, and there's your block!

For the next triangle turn your ruler so that same horizontal line is on your top stitching line.

Continue down the tube to get as many triangles as you can from a strip set.

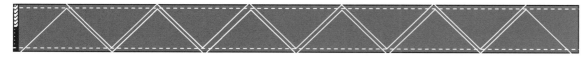

Read on for more information on ᵀʰᵉ Strip Tube Ruler™, including what to do if you don't have one.

Making Half Square Triangles

Did you notice that The **Strip Tube Ruler**™ makes pieced Half Square Triangles? That means you can make regular Half Square Triangles too!

For Half Square Triangles, your tube needs to be just two fabrics cut the same width. Here's a great chart to help you cut your strips. It is based on fabric 40" wide with little fabric waste between cuts.

Finished Block Size	Cut Size (and Ruler Measurement)	Width of Tube	Yield per Strip Set
1 ½"	2"	1 ¾" wide	23 Blocks
2"	2 ½"	2" wide	18 Blocks
2 ½"	3"	2 ½" wide	16 Blocks
3"	3 ½"	3" wide	14 Blocks
3 ½"	4"	3 ¼" wide	12 Blocks
4"	4 ½"	3 ½" wide	10 Blocks
4 ½"	5"	4" wide	9 Blocks
5"	5 ½"	4 ¼" wide	8 Blocks
5 ½"	6"	4 ¾" wide	8 Blocks
6"	6 ½"	5" wide	7 Blocks
6 ½"	7"	5 ½" wide	6 Blocks
7"	7 ½"	5 ¾" wide	6 Blocks
7 ½"	8"	6 ¼" wide	6 Blocks
8"	8 ½"	6 ½" wide	5 Blocks
8 ½"	9"	6 ¾" wide	5 Blocks
9"	9 ½ "	7 ¼" wide	4 Blocks

For example, to get a finished Half Square Triangle Block that finishes 4" square, sew a dark strip with a width of 3 ½" together with a light strip with a width of 3 ½" to make a tube. Use the 4 ½" measurement on The **Strip Tube Ruler**™ to cut out triangles that open to 4 ½" squares. You will get 10 blocks per strip set. When sewn together, those blocks will finish at 4" square.

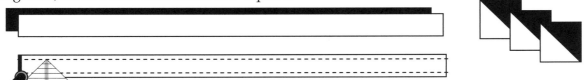

Tip: You will have bias edges, so follow the tips on the next page to help keep your edges from stretching.

Freestyle:
You can also create your own design using strips of various sizes. Just make sure your strip set is at least as wide as the tube size listed in the chart above. And please note that if it is much bigger than listed, you might not get as many blocks out of a strip set as listed.

4

Tips Using the Strip Tube Technique

General Points

- The measurement on the ruler will be your the unfinished block size. For example, if you use the 5 ½" measurement you are cutting a 5 ½" square which will finish at 5".
- Guess what… you are squaring up your blocks as you cut! Yeah!
- Before sewing your tube together, make sure your strip sets are the same width. <u>Slight</u> differences now and then can be compensated by sewing your quarter inch seam off of the shorter edge. Just be sure you still have almost ¼" of fabric in the seam allowance to maintain the quilt integrity.
- When making your tube, keep the fabrics flat so you don't create bubbles or gaps in your tube.
- If you have a few stitches in the top corner, just pull them out before opening it to a square.
- Make fresh cuts with each triangle to keep it true. Stay as close to the previous cut as possible to conserve fabric.
- You can cut any size square from your tube as long as there is fabric under the ruler to make it a complete block. In other words, the point of the ruler doesn't need to go all the way to the top of the tube.
- If you know what size block you want, use the chart on the previous page to make the appropriate tube size.
- You are working with bias edges, so be sure you don't stretch your blocks when you sew them together. We also advise that you don't press with steam as that will warp the edges. Some of our strip clubbers use sizing or spray starch to give keep it from stretching too much.

Another Option

If you don't have ^{The} Strip Tube Ruler™, you can use a square-up ruler. Turn it so the 0 point is on the top. Find your measurement down the left and down the right side of the ruler (9" in our example to the right.) Mark it with masking tape. Use the marks on the ruler as your cutting guide.

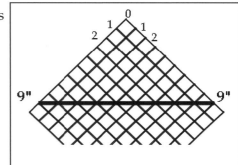

General Sewing Information

General points

- Use a sharp blade in your rotary cutter and a fresh needle in your machine.
- Sew a consistent scant ¼" seam. That means sew a seam a thread smaller than ¼" so that when you fold the fabric, you'll have the correct finished size. To check your seam, sew three 2 ½" strips together. They should measure 6 ½" from edge to edge. If they don't, adjust your seam until they do.

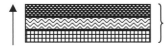 } Three strips sewn together should measure 6 ½" wide.

- The arrow indicates pressing direction. In the example above, you need to press the seams up.
- Avoid using steam on bias edges.

Borders

To get the best results with borders, you should cut your border fabric to the size of your quilt. That means measuring your quilt before attaching the borders. If, like me, you usually attach your borders to the left and right sides first, then to the top and bottom, you first need to measure the length of the quilt. Do this in three places- the left edge, the middle and the right edge. If they are different (which they usually are to a degree) take the average of the three measurements. Now piece and/or cut your border strips so you get two long strips of the length measurement. Attach to the left and right. Next measure the new width in three places just as you did with the length. Piece and/or cut border strips so you get two long strips of that width measurement. Attach to the top and bottom. Repeat this process for the other borders.

Layer, Quilt and Bind

Layer, Quilt, and Bind are our favorite three words. It means a quilt top is done. But what else does it mean?

- "Layer" means that you need to make a sandwich with the backing on the bottom facing down, the batting in the middle and the pieced quilt on top facing up. Make sure the batting and backing are larger than the top so you have some wiggle room during quilting. Baste or pin the three together, making sure there are no pleats or bubbles in either the top or the back.
- "Quilt" means that you stitch through all three layers to hold the quilt together and keep the batting in place. You can do it yourself or you can have a professional quilter do it for you. If you have a professional quilter do it, you might not have to baste or pin the layers. Check with the quilter.
- "Bind" means that you add fabric to the outside of the quilt to finish the raw edges. My favorite binding technique follows.

Binding

Cut 2 ½" strips from Width of Fabric (WOF).
Sew the strips together at a 45° angle to create one long strip. Cut away excess fabric and press open.

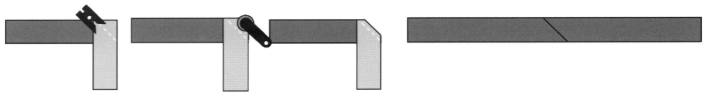

With the wrong side facing you, fold over the first corner as pictured to create a triangle at the end. Then fold the strip up lengthwise and press.

Using a ¼" seam, sew the binding to the top side of the sandwich leaving the first 5-6 inches of the binding unsewn (A). Start by backstitching and stop when you are ¼" from the end (B). Backstitch again.

Turn the binding strip up to get a 45° crease (C) then back down again so the second fold is flush with the top of the quilt (D). For the next seam, start about half an inch down, backstitch to the edge and sew forward again until you are a ¼" from the end. Backstitch and repeat steps C and D.

Complete all four corners.

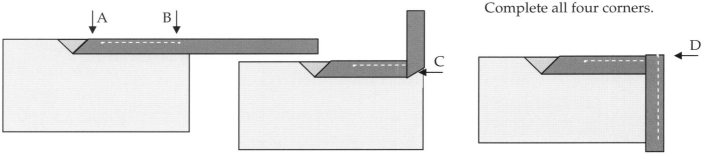

When you get back to where you started, fold the binding (E) so you have a finished edge that fits just under the 45° lip. Cut away excess fabric. Tuck under the lip and sew all of the layers to finish attaching the binding.

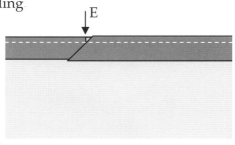

Trim away excess batting.

Turn the binding over to the back and blind stitch by hand. Your mitered corners should just flip into place.

Freestyle Roman Stripes

Designed by
Daniela Stout

Fabric Requirements for 2 ½" strips

Finished sizes may vary	**Lap** 48" x 64"	**Larger Throw** 64" x 80"	**Queen** 96" x 96"	**King** 112" x 112"
Block Arrangements	*6 x 8*	*8 x 10*	*12 x 12*	*14 x 14*
2 ½" strips x WOF of various fabrics	30 — 2 ½" strips *or 10— ¼ yard cuts*	48— 2 ½" strips *or 16— ¼ yard cuts*	87— 2 ½" strips *or 29 — ¼ yard cuts*	120— 2 ½" strips *or 40— ¼ yard cuts*
Background	2 yards	3 ⅛yards	5 ½ yards	7 ⅝yards
Binding	½ yards (6— 2 ½" strips)	⅝yards (8— 2 ½" strips)	¾ yards (10— 2 ½" strips)	⅞yards (12— 2 ½" strips)
Backing	3 yards	4 ⅞yards	8 ⅔ yards	10 yards

Note: See next page for fabric requirements for 1 ½" strips options!

Strips and Background

If you don't already have print strips, cut them now from width of fabric.

You will need 30— 2 ½" strips (48, 87, 120).

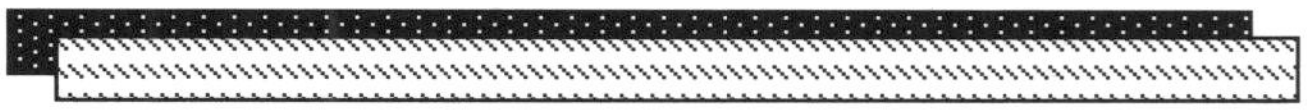

From your background, cut 10—6 ½" strips (16, 29, 40).

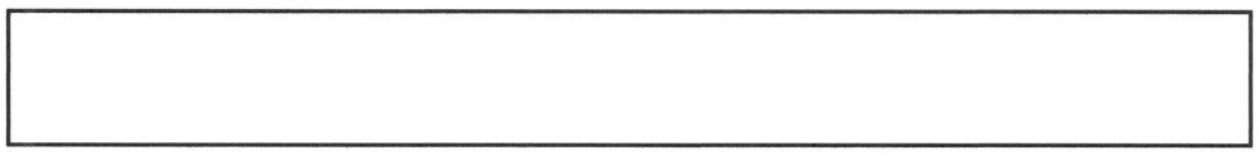

Making the Block

Sew three print strips together. Press in one direction. Repeat to make 10 strip sets (16, 29, 40) measuring 6 ½" wide.

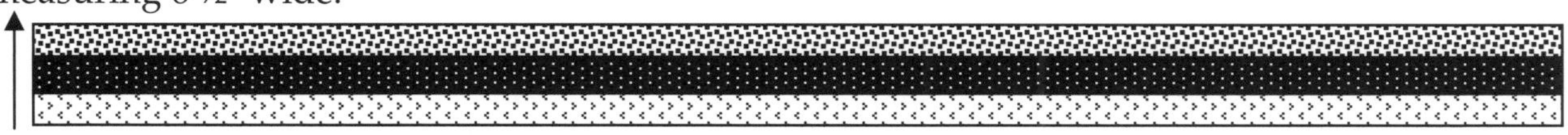

On one of the strip sets, place a 6 ½" background strip right sides together. Sew a ¼" seam on the top and the bottom to make a tube.

¼" seam on top and

Using the technique outlined in the beginning of this book. Cut out 5—8 ½" squares from each strip set. If you are lucky enough to get 6 per strip set, you can make your quilt bigger!

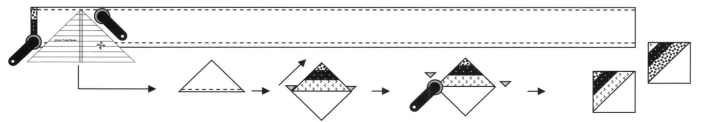

Make a total of 48 Blocks with (80, 144, 196) measuring 8 ½" square.

or Fabric Requirements for 1 ½" strips

Finished sizes may vary	Baby 30" x 40"	Lap 40" x 50"	Throw 60" x 70"	Queen 100" x 100"
Block Arrangements	6 x 8	8 x 10	12 x 14	20 x 20
1 ½" strips x WOF of various fabrics	24 — 1 ½" strips or 5— ¼ yard cuts	36— 1 ½" strips or 8— ¼ yard cuts	76— 1 ½" strips or 16 ¼ yard cuts	180— 1 ½" strips or 36— ¼ yard cuts
Background	⅞ yards	1 ¼ yards	2 ½ yards	6 yards
Binding	⅓ yards (4— 2 ½" strips)	⅜ yards (5— 2 ½" strips)	⅝ yards (7— 2 ½" strips)	⅞ yards (11— 2 ½" strips)
Backing	1 ⅓ yards	2 yards 	3 ¾ yards 	9 yards 

Strips should be at least 42" width of fabric (WOF).

Note: See previous page for fabric requirements for 2 ½" strips options!

Strips and Background

If you don't already have print strips, cut them now from width of fabric.

You will need 24— 1 ½" strips (36, 76, 180).

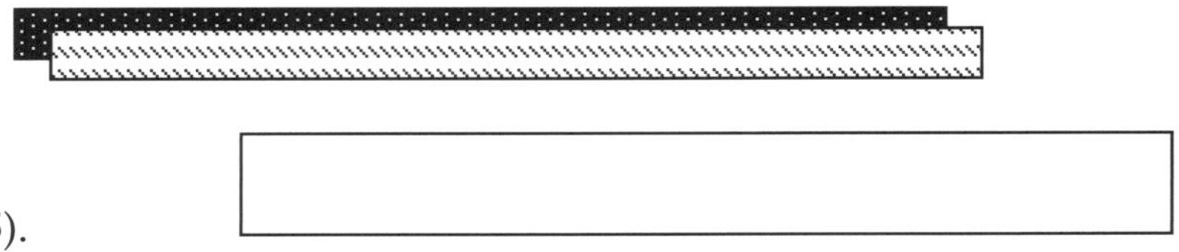

From your background, cut 6—4 ½" strips (9, 19, 45).

Making the Block

Sew four print strips together. Press in one direction. Repeat to make 6 strip sets (9, 19, 45) measuring 4 ½" wide.

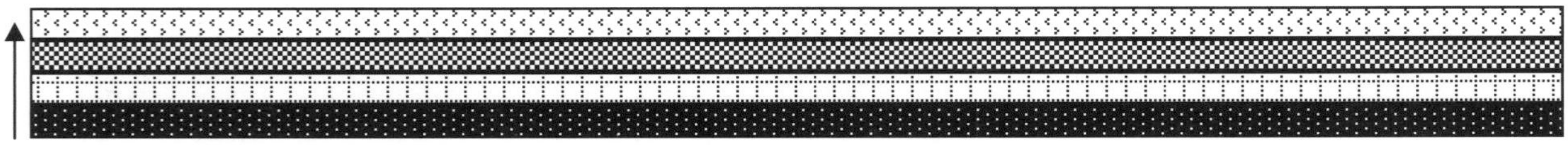

On one of the strip sets, place a 4 ½" background strip right sides together. Sew a ¼" seam on the top and the bottom to make a tube.

Using the technique outlined in the beginning of this book. Cut out 9—5 ½" squares from each strip set.

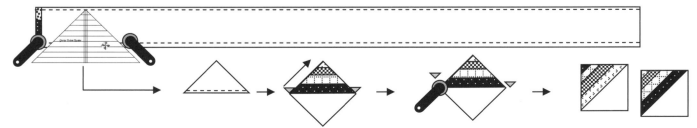

Make a total of 48 Blocks with (80, 168, 400) measuring 5 ½" square.

Layout

Now that you have your blocks, twist and turn them to achieve your own quilt design. There are so many potential layouts that we can't even show them all. Below are some of my favorite options for the 6 x 8 arrangements.

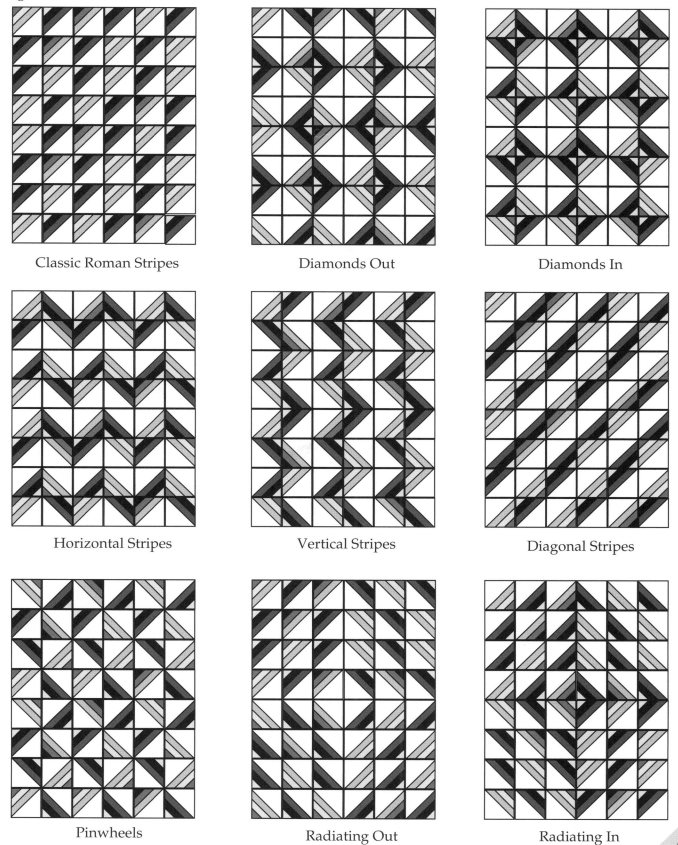

Classic Roman Stripes   Diamonds Out   Diamonds In

Horizontal Stripes   Vertical Stripes   Diagonal Stripes

Pinwheels   Radiating Out   Radiating In

Double Star

Designed by
Georgette
Dell'Orco

Fabric Requirements

Finished sizes may vary	**Baby** 46" x 56"	**Throw** 56" x 66"	**Twin** 76" x 96"	**Queen** 96" x 106"
Block Arrangements	*3 x 4*	*4 x 5*	*6 x 8*	*8 x 9*
2 ½" strips x WOF of various fabrics	12 — 2 ½" strips or 4— ¼ yard cuts	20— 2 ½" strips or 7— ¼ yard cuts	44— 2 ½" strips or 15— ¼ yard cuts	64— 2 ½" strips or 22— ¼ yard cuts
Light Background	½ yard	⅔ yard	1 ½ yards	2 ⅛ yards
Medium Background	½ yard	⅔ yard	1 ½ yards	2 ⅛ yards
Border 1	⅜ yard	½ yard	⅔ yard	¾ yards
Border 2	1 yards	1 ⅓ yards	2 yards	2 ⅛ yards
Binding	½ yard (6— 2 ½" strips)	⅝ yard (7— 2 ½" strips)	⅔ yard (9— 2 ½" strips)	⅞ yard (11— 2 ½" strips)
Backing	2 ⅔ yards	3 ⅝ yards	7 yards	9 ½ yards

Strips and Background

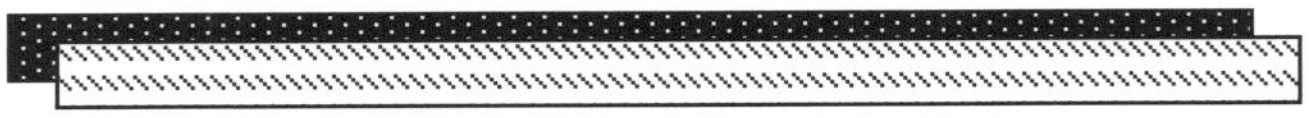

If you don't already have print strips, cut them now from width of fabric.

You will need 12— 2 ½" strips (20, 44, 64).

From your light background, cut 3—4 ½" strips (5, 11, 16).

From your medium background, cut 3—4 ½" strips (5, 11, 16).

Strips should be at least 42" width of fabric (WOF).

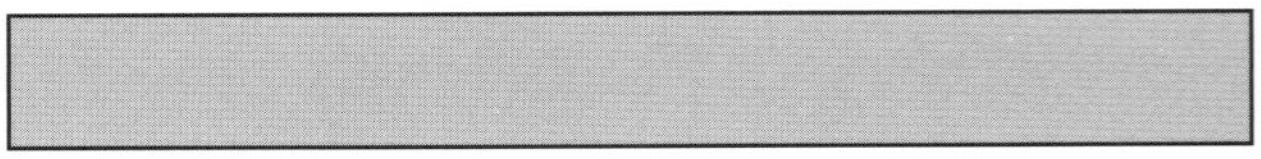

Making the Smaller Block

Sew two print strips together. Press in one direction. Repeat to make 6 strip sets (10, 22, 32) measuring 4 ½" wide.

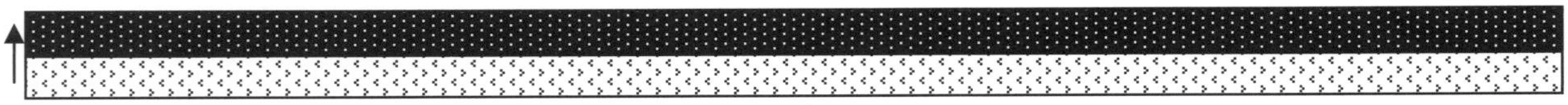

On one of the strip sets, place a 4 ½" light background strip right sides together. Sew a ¼" seam on the top and the bottom to make a tube.

¼" seam on top and bottom

Place the 5 ½" measurement of you're ᵀʰᵉ Strip Tube Ruler™ on the <u>bottom stitching line</u>. Cut out a triangle that opens to a 5 ½" square. Press away from the background. Trim off dog ears.

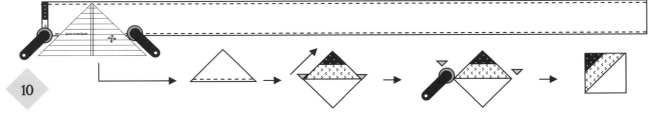

Making the Block (continued)

Repeat with the 5 ½" measurement on the <u>top stitching line</u>, making fresh cuts. Open to get another 5 ½" square. Press away from the background. Trim off dog ears. Continue down the strip set to get 9 squares from each strip set.

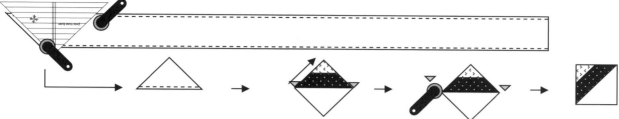

Repeat for 3 strip sets (5, 11, 16) with Light Background.

<u>Make a total of 24 Blocks with Light Background (40, 96, 144).</u>

Now do the same thing with Medium Background. This time press towards the background.

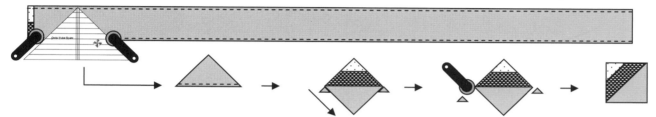

<u>Make a total of 24 Blocks with Medium Background (40, 96, 144).</u>

Making the Larger Block

Mix and match fabrics and pull two square with Light Background and two with Medium Background. Assemble as pictured to make your Larger Block.

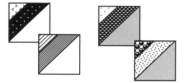 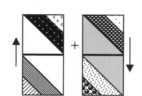 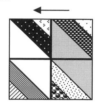

<u>Make a total of 12 Large Blocks (20, 48, 72)</u>
<u>Measuring 10 ½"</u>

Assembling

Twist and turn your blocks so your quilt matches the diagram on the next page.

Sew your blocks together by rows. Then sew your rows together to make the quilt. Press the first row in one direction, and the second row in the other direction. Repeat with all of the other rows.

Below is an example of Row 1 of the Twin.

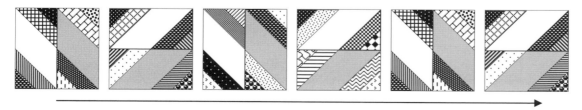

Finishing

From your Border 1 Fabric, cut 5—2 ½" strips (6, 9, 10) Attach to quilt.
From your Border 2 Fabric, cut 5— 6 ½" strips (7, 10, 11). Attach to quilt.

Layer, Quilt and Bind.

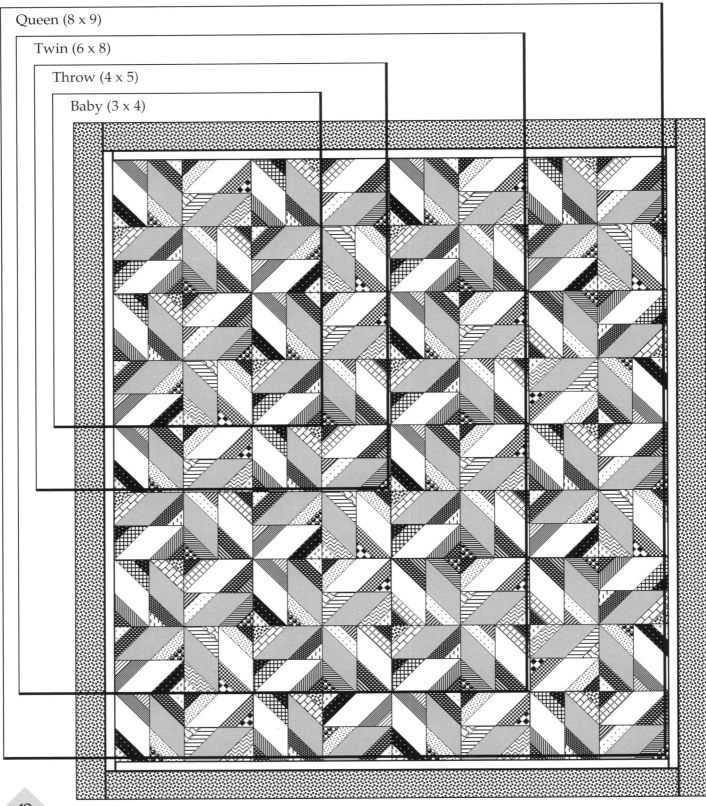

Queen (8 x 9)

Twin (6 x 8)

Throw (4 x 5)

Baby (3 x 4)

Double Star

Designed by: Georgette Dell'Orco

Twin Pictured

**Freestyle Roman Stripes
with 2½" strips**
Designed by: Daniela Stout
Large Throw Pictured

**Freestyle Roman Stripes
with 1 ½" strips**
Designed by: Daniela Stout
Throw Pictured

Cozy Quilt Designs™

Cut Diamonds

Designed by: Daniela Stout
Throw Pictured

One Ruler. So Many Possibilities!
The **Strip Tube Ruler**™
by Cozy Quilt Designs™

Quilter and Piecer Credits

Double Star was pieced by Claudia Harper and quilted by Liz Henselmeier. **Bear Paw Star** was pieced by Andrew Resnik. **Cut Diamonds** was pieced by Jan Hayman. **Freestyle Roman Stripes with 1½" Strips** was pieced by Claudia Harper. **Freestyle Roman Stripes with 2½" Strips** was pieced by Lisa Molitor and quilted by Liz Henselmeier. **Just Too Easy** was pieced by Carrie Meth and quilted by Lorrie Ayala.

Just Too Easy

Designed by: Susan Van Alyne
Throw Pictured

Bear Paw Star

Designed by: Daniela Stout
Large Throw Pictured

◆ Cozy Quilt Designs™

Just Too Easy!

Designed by Susan Van Alyne

Susan works at *The Quilt House, Inc.* in Gardnerville, Nevada where she uses and loves The Strip Tube Ruler™!

Fabric Requirements

Finished sizes may vary	**Throw** 52" x 62"	**Twin** 72" x 92"	**Queen** 92" x 92"	**King** 102" x 102"
Block Arrangements	*4 x 5*	*6 x 8*	*8 x 8*	*9 x 9*
2 ½" strips x WOF of various fabrics	40 — 2 ½" strips *or 14— ¼ yard cuts*	96— 2 ½" strips *or 32— ¼ yard cuts*	128— 2 ½" strips *or 43— ¼ yard cuts*	164— 2 ½" strips *or 55— ¼ yard cuts*
Border 1	½ yard	⅔ yard	¾ yards	¾ yards
Border 2	1 yard	1 ¼ yards	1 ⅓ yards	1 ½ yards
Binding	½ yards (6— 2 ½" strips)	⅔ yards (9— 2 ½" strips)	¾ yards (10— 2 ½" strips)	⅞ yards (11— 2 ½" strips)
Backing	3 yards 	5 ⅝ yards 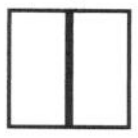	7 yards 	9 ¼ yards 

Strips and Background

If you don't already have print strips, cut them now from width of fabric.

    You will need 40— 2 ½" strips (96, 128, 164).

Making the Block

Sew two <u>contrasting</u> print strips together. Press in one direction. Repeat to make 20 strip sets (48, 64, 81) measuring 4 ½" wide.

Place two strip sets right sides together so the seams nest. Sew a ¼" seam on the top and the bottom to make a tube. Make 10 tubes (24, 32, 41).

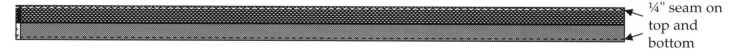

¼" seam on top and bottom

Place the 5 ½" measurement of your The Strip Tube Ruler™ on the <u>bottom stitching line</u>. Cut out a triangle that opens to a 5 ½" square. Press all seams in the same direction. Trim off dog ears.

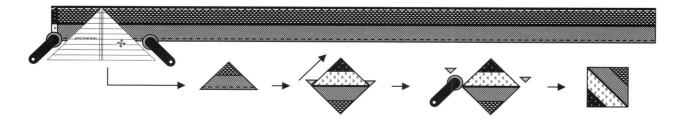

Making the Block (continued)

Repeat with the 5 ½" measurement on the <u>top stitching line</u>, making fresh cuts. Open to get another 5 ½" square. Press all seams in the same direction. Trim off dog ears.

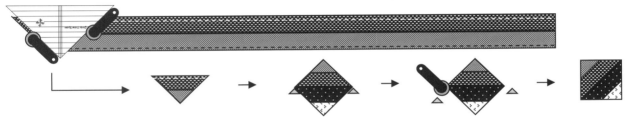

Continue down the strip set to get 8 squares with two different fabric configurations from each strip set. (Note: you might get 9 squares from each set, but you only need 8 for the blocks.)

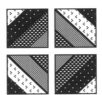

Pulling two blocks of each configuration, arrange them so that they create an alternating pattern in the middle. Sew them together. The seams should nest. This is your block!

Repeat so the *other* colors come together in the center to create the alternating pattern. You will get two blocks from each strip set.

<u>Make a total of 20 Blocks (48, 64, 81) measuring 10 ½" square.</u>

Finishing

Arrange your blocks in a pleasing manner and sew your blocks together by rows. Then sew your rows together to get your quilt. The block arrangement without borders for the Throw is below. Turn to the next page for other layouts.

From your Border 1 Fabric, cut 6—2 ½" strips (9, 10, 10). Attach to quilt.
From your Border 2 Fabric, cut 7—4 ½" strips (9, 10, 11). Attach to quilt.

Layer, Quilt and Bind.

A Personal Note:
I designed this block one lovely fall afternoon. My husband was taking a rare nap on the couch. I loved the way the block just fell together so much that I actually woke him up to show him!

Then I decided to name it after myself, so I call this the Daniela Block!

Susan from *The Quilt House, Inc.* in Gardnerville, Nevada put it together in this great quilt layout and was kind enough to let us use it in this book.

Thank you, Susan!

Daniela Stout
Cozy Quilt Designs

Layout

Below is a layout diagram for all of the quilts. We used shading so you can better see the design.

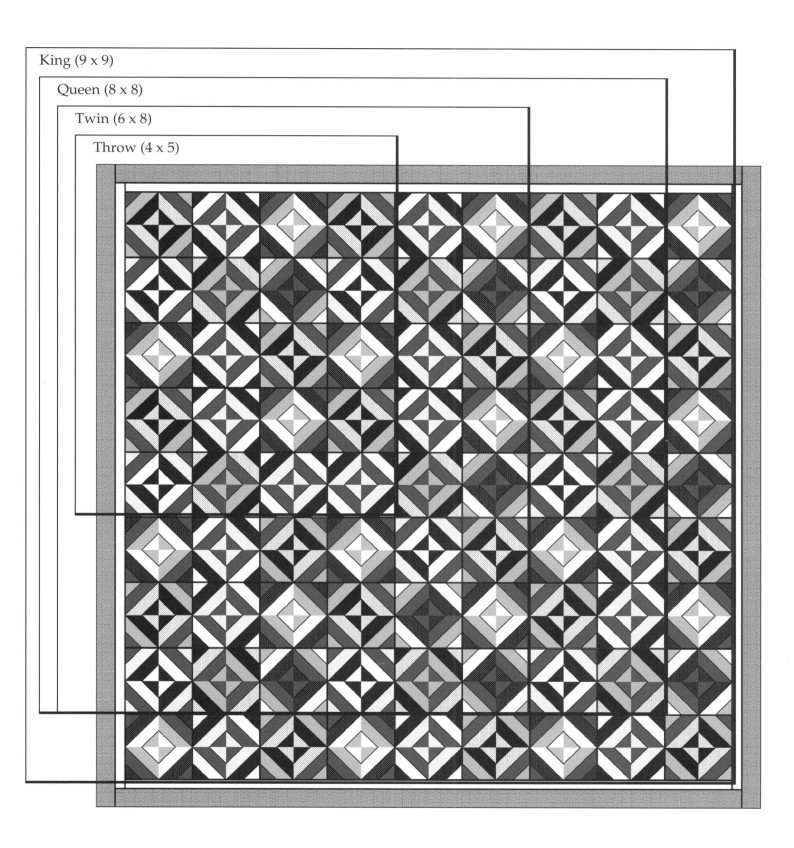

King (9 x 9)

Queen (8 x 8)

Twin (6 x 8)

Throw (4 x 5)

19

Bear Paw Star

Designed by
Daniela Stout

Fabric Requirements

Finished sizes may vary	Large Throw 76" x 76"	Twin 76" x 92"	Queen 92" x 92"	King 108" x 108"
Block Arrangements	*8 x 8*	*8 x 10*	*10 x 10*	*12 x 12*
2 ½" strips x WOF of various fabrics	42 — 2 ½" strips or 14 — ¼ yard cuts	54 — 2 ½" strips or 18 — ¼ yard cuts	78 — 2 ½" strips or 26 — ¼ yard cuts	102 — 2 ½" strips or 34 — ¼ yard cuts
Background	2 ⅓ yard	2 ⅔ yard	3 ⅛ yards	4 ⅞ yards
Border 1	⅝ yard	⅔ yard	¾ yard	⅞ yard
Border 2	1 ⅛ yards	1 ¼ yards	1 ⅓ yards	1 ⅝ yards
Binding	⅝ yard (8 — 2 ½" strips)	⅔ yard (9 — 2 ½" strips)	¾ yard (10 — 2 ½" strips)	⅞ yards (12 — 2 ½" strips)
Backing	5 ⅞ yards	5 ⅞ yards	7 yards	9 ¾ yards

Strips and Background

If you don't already have print strips, cut them now from width of fabric.

You will need 42 — 2 ½" strips (54, 78, 102)

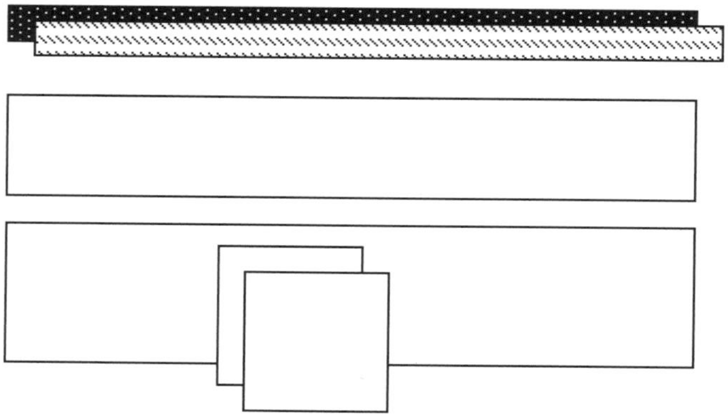

From your Background
cut 8 — 6 ½" strips (10, 12, 20) and
cut 3 — 8 ½" strips (3, 3, 4) then cut those into
12 — 8 ½" squares (12, 12, 16).

Making the Block A

Sew three print strips together. Press in one direction.
Repeat to make 14 strip sets (18, 26, 34) measuring 6 ½" wide.

Pair a strip set with a background strip of 6 ½". Place right sides together and sew a ¼" seam on the top and the bottom to make a tube. Make 8 tubes (10, 12, 20).

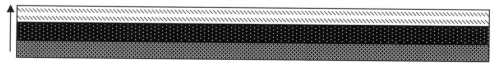

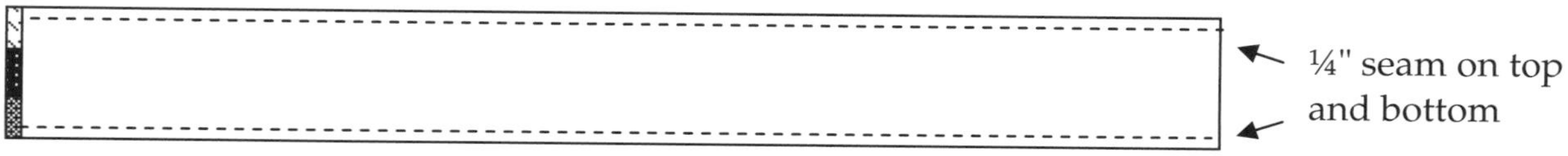

← ¼" seam on top
and bottom

Making Block A (continued)

Place the 8 ½" measurement of ^{The} Strip Tube Ruler™ on the <u>bottom stitching line</u>. Cut out a triangle that opens to a 8 ½" square. Press away from the background. Trim off dog ears.

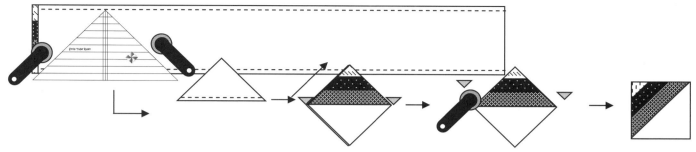

Repeat with the 8 ½" measurement on the <u>top stitching line</u>, making fresh cuts. Open to get another 8 ½" square. Press away from the background. Trim off dog ears. Continue down the strip set to get 5 squares from each strip set. If you get 6 squares per strip set , you can either make your quilt larger or save them for another project!

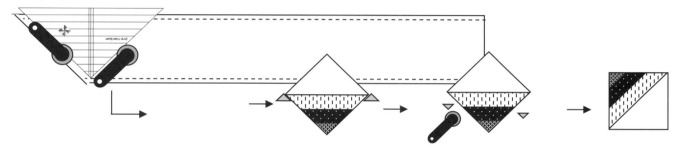

<u>Repeat for all 8 tubes (10, 12, 20) to make a total of 40 Block A's (48, 56, 96).</u>

Making Block B

Place two of the remaining strip sets right sides together so the seams nest. Sew ¼" seam on the top and ¼" seam on the bottom to make another tube. Repeat to make 3 tubes (4, 7, 7).

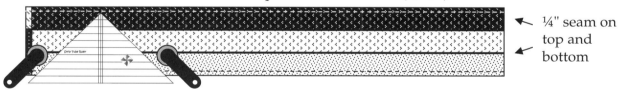

← ¼" seam on top and bottom

Using the same technique and measurement as above, cut out 5— 8 ½" squares from each tube.

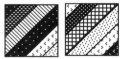

<u>Repeat for all 3 tubes (4, 7, 7) to make a total of 12 Block B's (20, 32, 32).</u>

Assembling the Quilt Top

On the next two pages, you will find layouts of the different quilt sizes. To make it easier to differentiate the blocks, we've shaded them by Block A, Block B and the background block.

Carefully layout your quilt. You may choose to arrange your blocks differently, but try to keep it symmetrical.

Sew your blocks together by rows, alternating your pressing for each row. Then sew your rows together to get your quilt top.

Tip: Consider visualizing the quilt layout by quadrants.
When you only have to concentrate on quarter of the quilt at a time, it become simpler. To the right is a plain graphic of the King layout sectioned off into quarters as an example.

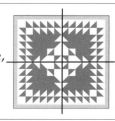

Assembling the Quilt Top (continued)

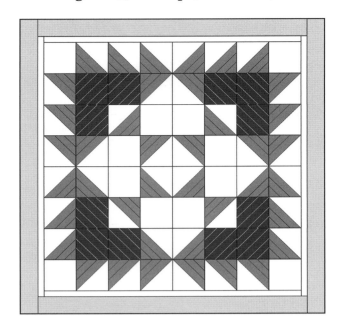

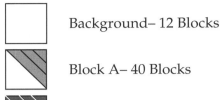

Throw

Background– 12 Blocks

Block A– 40 Blocks

Block B– 12 Blocks

Twin

Background– 12 Blocks

Block A– 48 Blocks

Block B– 20 Blocks

From your Border 1 Fabric, cut 8—2 ½" strips (9, 10, 11) Attach to quilt.
From your Border 2 Fabric, cut 8— 4 ½" strips (9, 10, 12). Attach to quilt.

Layer, Quilt and Bind.

Assembling the Quilt Top (continued)

Queen

 Background– 12 Blocks

Block A– 56 Blocks

Block B– 32 Blocks

King

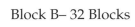 Background– 16 Blocks

Block A– 96 Blocks

Block B– 32 Blocks

Cut Diamonds

Designed by
Daniela Stout

Fabric Requirements

Finished sizes may vary	**Throw** 55" x 68"	**Twin** 68" x 94"	**Queen** 94" x 94"	**King** 107" x 107"
Block Arrangements	*6 x 8*	*8 x 12*	*12 x 12*	*14 x 14*
2 ½" strips x WOF of various fabrics	32 — 2 ½" strips *or 11— ¼ yard cuts*	64— 2 ½" strips *or 22— ¼ yard cuts*	96— 2 ½" strips *or 32— ¼ yard cuts*	132— 2 ½" strips *or 44— ¼ yard cuts*
Light Background	½ yard	1 yard	1 ½ yards	2 yards
Dark Background	½ yard	1 yard	1 ½ yards	2 yards
Border 1	⅜yard	⅝yard	¾ yard	¾ yards
Border 2	⅓ yards	⅜yard	½ yards	½ yards
Border 3	1 ⅛yards	1 ⅓ yards	1 ⅔ yards	1 ⅞yards
Binding	⅝yard (7— 2 ½" strips)	⅔ yard (9— 2 ½" strips)	¾ yard (10— 2 ½" strips)	⅞yard (11— 2 ½" strips)
Backing	3 ½ yards	5 ⅞yards	8 ½ yards	9 ½ yards

Strips and Background

Strips should be at least 42" width of fabric (WOF).

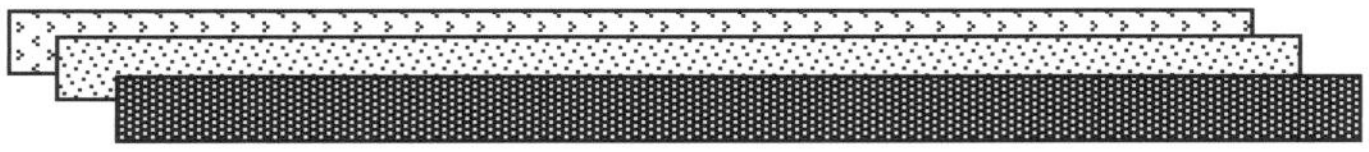

If you don't already have print strips, cut them now from width of fabric.

  You will need 32— 2 ½" strips (64, 96, 132).

From your light background, cut 8—2" strips (16, 24, 33).
From your dark background, cut 8—2" strips (16, 24, 33).

Making the Strip Sets

Sew a print strip to each side of a Dark Background strip. Press in one direction.
Repeat to make 8 strip sets (16, 24, 33).

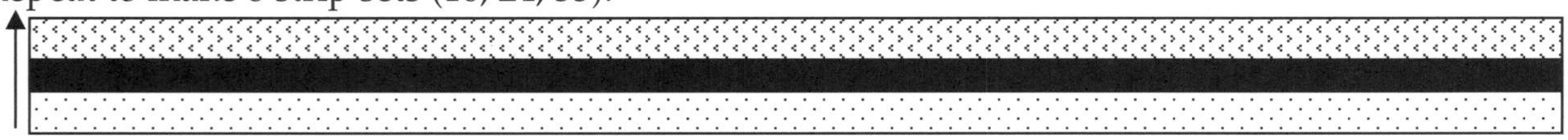

Sew a print strip to each side of a Light Background strip. Press in one direction.
Repeat to make 8 strip sets (16, 24, 33).

Place a Dark Background Strip Set on top of a Light Background Strip Set so the raw edges line up and the seams nest. Sew a ¼" seam on the top and the bottom to make a tube. Make 8 tubes (16, 24, 33).

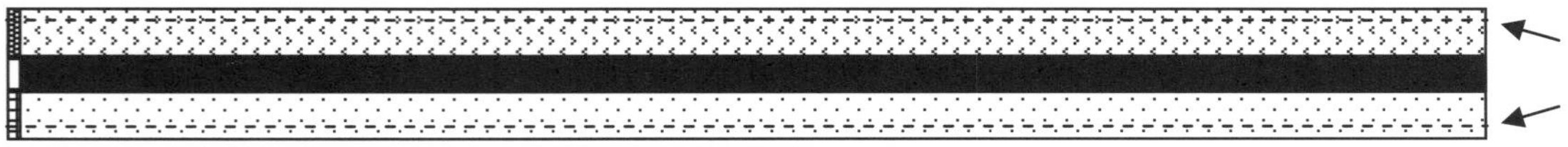

← ¼" seam on top and bottom

24

Making the Block

Place the 7" measurement of ^{The} Strip Tube Ruler ™ on the <u>bottom stitching line</u>. Cut out a triangle that opens to a 7" square. Press the large seam in the same direction as the other seams. Trim off dog ears.

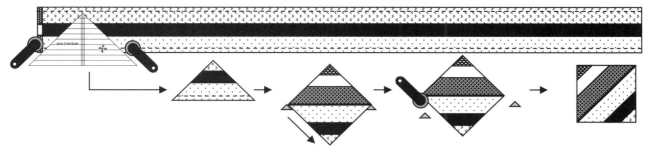

Repeat with the 7" measurement on the <u>top stitching line</u>, making fresh cuts. Open to get another 7" square. Press the large seam in the same direction as the other seams. Trim off dog ears. Continue down the strip set to get 6 squares from each strip set.

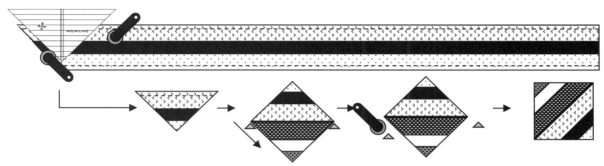

<u>Repeat for 8 tubes (16, 24, 33) and make a total of 48 Blocks (96, 144, 196).</u>

Assembling the Quilt Top

On the next pages are two possible layouts for this quilt. To make it easier to see the pattern, we've shaded the blocks so the Dark and the Light Background fabrics stand out.

Notice that four smaller blocks make a larger block and that there are two different larger blocks in each quilt.

<u>Quilt Blocks for Option 1</u>

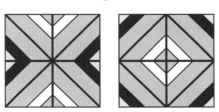

<u>Quilt Blocks for Option 2</u>

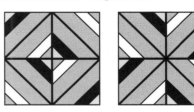

Arrange the blocks to achieve the pattern. In both options, Row 1 starts with the block on the left, then alternates with the block on the right. The second row then begins with the block on the right and alternates with the block on the left.

Once you have your layout, sew your blocks together by rows. Then sew your rows together to get the quilt.

Finishing

From your Border 1 Fabric, cut 5— 2 ½" strips (8, 9, 10) Attach to quilt.
From your Border 2 Fabric, cut 6— 1 ½" strips (8, 10, 10). Attach to quilt.
From your Border 3 Fabric, cut 7— 5 ½" strips (8, 10, 11). Attach to quilt.

Layer, Quilt and Bind.

Layout Option 1

Note that the quilt is essentially two larger blocks made out of the smaller blocks. (Pictured to the right.) Alternate the larger blocks as pictured below.

 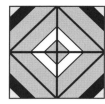

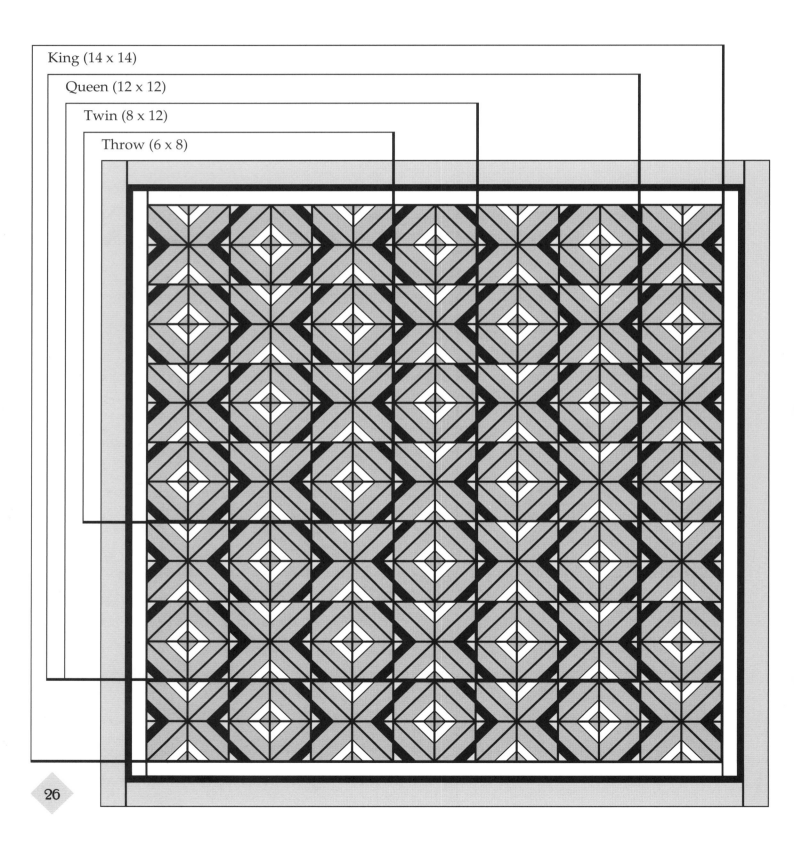

King (14 x 14)

Queen (12 x 12)

Twin (8 x 12)

Throw (6 x 8)

Layout Option 2

Note that the quilt is essentially two larger blocks made out of the smaller blocks. (Pictured to the right.) Alternate the larger blocks as pictured below.

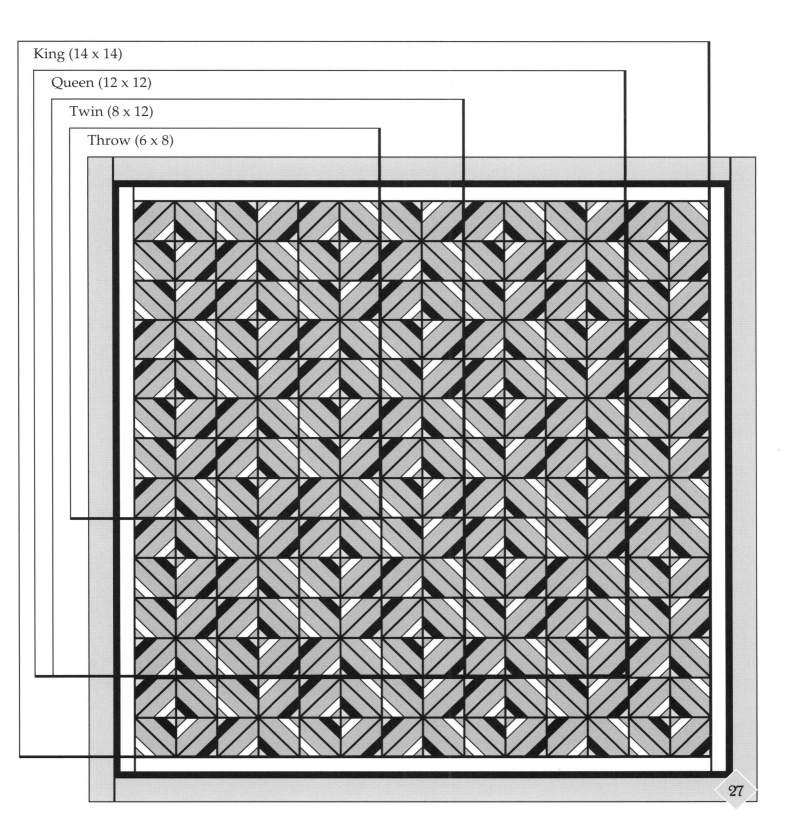

King (14 x 14)

Queen (12 x 12)

Twin (8 x 12)

Throw (6 x 8)

Cozy Quilt Designs

Cozy Quilt Designs™ is the publisher of numerous books including the best-selling titles, **Strip Clubbing**, and **More Strip Clubbing.**

We have also published over 100 patterns. Many of them for 2 ½" strips, fat quarters, and charm squares.

We test each of our patterns 2 to 4 times before it is published. Sometimes errors or typos still sneak by. Check our website for any corrections.

As you know, we also created ᵀʰᵉ Strip Tube Ruler™. Ask for it by name!

Cozy Quilt Shop

Cozy Quilt Designs is the publishing side of Cozy Quilt Shop. If you are in the San Diego area, make sure you stop by! We have 4,500 square feet of brightly-lit retail space and over 3,000 bolts of quality fabric.

We love events and hold Cake Therapy (in honor of pre-cut 10" squares) and Strip Club (in honor of pre-cut 2 ½" strips) monthly.

At each of these events, we unveil a new fabulous pattern. It's great fun!

Check us out.

Cozy Quilt Shop
2940 Jamacha Road, Suite H
El Cajon, CA 92019 USA
619-670-0652

And visit us online at CozyQuilt.com.